GW00707857

To Mum, With Love

Poems by Janet Beardsall
Illustrations by Averil Gilkes

This book is dedicated to
women and mothers everywhere
in the hope that they will share
some of the thoughts and emotions
expressed in these poems.

First published in 2007 by
Janet Beardsall
Melverley, Lower Broad Oak Road, West Hill,
Ottery St Mary, Devon, EX11 1UF

Printed by Creeds The Printers
Broad Oak, Bridport, Dorset, DT6 5NL

ISBN 978-0-9550796-1-0

Because
(For Averil)

Today it's better
Because there's sunshine
      birdsong
       spring flowers
But mostly because
       there's you.

Front cover: painting by Averil of her daughter Lara, age 4

To Mum, With Love

Contents

Hospiscare can do so much more than just relieve the symptoms of a life-threatening illness. We can help patients live their lives. More than that we can take the fear out of people's situation, and help them to find peace of mind.

The words we hear from patients and those close to them are 'reassurance', 'understanding' and 'hope'. These words help to illustrate the very real difference Hospiscare can make.

Hospiscare believe that the last chapter of people's lives is of high value. We treat every patient as an individual, personalising our care to each person's needs. We also provide support for the whole family and carers too.

Hospiscare operates in Exeter, and mid and east Devon. We provide specialist nurses who visit patients at home, give medical advice and emotional support, a hospice for 24 hour care, as well as working with and training other health professionals.

Our service is provided free to all those who need it. We need £3.8m a year to maintain all our services. Most of our funding is raised by the local community, giving a little to make a large difference.

For more information about Hospiscare visit our website www.hospiscare.co.uk Here you will find details about all our services, as well as opportunities to support our work.

Babies and Children

Battlefield

Pray for me
For tomorrow I'll be
Going into battle.

Agony
Maybe death there will be
In tomorrow's battle.

But I do
It for them and for you
Think of me in battle.

If I die
Tell them all it was my
Wish to die in battle.

Life is so
Gladly leave, freely go
Bravely fight in battle.

In childbed
Gambling life, facing death
Bringing life for battle.

Our own lives
For mankind, women give
Die for life, the battle.

Baby Books: Some Advice

"Baby needs feeding four hourly,
On the dot; don't you be late."
"Feed him whenever he wants, dear.
Don't let him get in a state."

"Don't always feed him at night-time."
"Always feed, if he should cry "
"Five times a day." "Three, I should say."
"Don't let him rule you, he'll try."

"Give him as much as he needs, dear."
"Don't let him have any more."
We'll do as we please. And as for all these,
I'm chucking the lot out the door!

Going Out

You wore a white coat
and a shocking pink hat
in the gold October sun.
How we laughed to each other

going along at a
cracking pace. We had a
one-sided conversation. I
talked a lot and you

listened intently and smiled
your beaming smile. You looked
lovely. How happy we felt as
you sat up for the first time
in your pram.

The Babysitter

Angie, dear, please stop that din!
Oh, hello, Ann. Do come in.
I'll just move this box of bricks
And this clockwork dog that ticks.
Pop your coat there on the floor
Putting hooks up's such a bore.
Don't do that to David, dear,
Leave the cat's tail, do you hear?
Have a seat, please Annie, do.
Now, what can I do for you?
I'll just look and see if we
Can manage that, I think we're free.
Now, where is my calendar?
Underneath the table? Ah!
Got it! In the washing pile,
Which has been there quite a while.
Sorry I can't give you tea
Run out of it – silly me.
Haven't made a cake for years
Busy on committees, dear.
David, don't swing on the door.
Or pour water on the floor.
Angie, don't write in that dust.
Going so soon? 'Scuse the fuss.
Trodden on a Rupert Bear?
David always leaves him there.
See you then on Saturday.
Move that trike, it's in your way.
Forget to come? Ha ha, that's good.
Forget things, me? — As if I would!

First Swim

Dithering by the edge
   Huddling, cowering,
Hovering on the ledge
   Hopping, shaking,
Half an hour of this
   Shivering, quivering,
Someone pushes her
   Crashing, splashing,
Into blue water
   Lapping, slapping.

Dear little daughter
   Waving, laughing,
Loves it in there so
   Bobbing, floating,
Doesn't want to go
   Shaking, pouting.
At last she is out
   Chatting, running,
And without a doubt
   Drying, dressing,
Next time she comes here
   Walking, combing,
She'll swim without fear
   Nodding, smiling.

Such Fun

"Don't feel right"
"Don't feel well"
"Can I go home, please?"

"Don't join in"
"Don't let him"
"Don't be such a tease."

"Don't like egg"
"Don't like ham"
"Don't want any cheese."

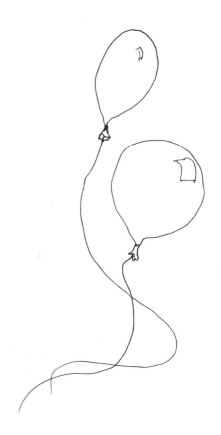

"Don't like puds"
"Don't like cakes"
"Can I be sick, please?"

"Don't like him"
"Don't like her"
"Don't want any Smarties."

"Don't like noise"
"Don't like games"
"I don't like kids' parties!"

A Lovely Day

"Goodbye, mother. Where's my lunch?"
"Seen my briefcase, dear?
Try to sit out in the sun,
Now that it is here."

Blearily she waved goodbye
As they drove away.
Went inside, broke up a fight,
Made the children play.

"Sit outside? – Well, yes I might –
James! – Now let me see,
Things I've got to do today –
First a cup of tea."

Then she started: fed the cat,
Hung the washing out,
Bathed the baby, rang the school,
Flicked some dust about.

Talked to Mrs.Borrowell
And her husband Fred,
Cleaned the windows, washed the floors,
Changed the eldest's bed.

Ironed the shirts and phoned the vet,
Drove down to the shops,
Made Jane's cakes, then played with Jim,
Shortened Susie's frocks.

Cooked the supper, washed the plates,
Bathed the youngest, read
Stories to them, heard theirs too,
Kissed them all in bed.

Listened to Sue's awful jokes,
Heard her bow and scrape,
Endured Prince's "Purple Rain"
Blasting from her tape.

"Oh, hello dear - yes, it's warm.
Had a lovely day?
Want your dinner? – In the sun?
Did it shine today?"

Golden Delicious

In the evening we picked the glowing apples
Gently twinting,
Carefully placing each one in a box.
Some fell with a thud
As we brushed aside the weighted branches
And the pale moths that lightly flitted past.
We chatted gaily under the rosy tree and rosy glowing sky.
Cider smells everywhere
And bonfires, grey-white smoke drifting over.

We stored the apples in a cool dark place,
Each one wrapped in a cosy coat,
So that when the cold dark days of winter come
We can unwrap the red glow of autumn
To taste golden September
And the warmth we shared, again.

Dragon Days

It's a dragon day today, she said,
As we stepped outside at nine
On a sunny but chill September day,
With cobwebs strung shimmering on display
Bead dresses hung out on a line.

We can see our breath today, she said,
In the golden gleaming air.
See it streams and it puffs like smoke grey-blue
I love it on dragon days, mum, don't you?
You can see that your breath is there.

Yes, it's like a puff of smoke, I said,
Watching breath make mini-fires.
But the dragons of time snuffed out the blaze
And gone is the glow of our dragon days
Like a little child's breath, expired.

Saying Goodbye

We hugged and kissed you. Said goodbye.
Waved you off down the road.
Returned to the house and closed the door.

It's too soon yet to tidy your room.
There's only silence behind your door
And such emptiness whiteness deadness.
I like the chaos of cups and glasses in
All the wrong places; the blizzard of
Clothes, shoes, books and CD's flung
Over the floor; and the riot of
Music, chat and mobile calls
Bursting from beneath the door.
And the light left on blazing like a beacon.
And the windows open letting out your warmth.

And it feels too soon to open this newly-closed door
To witness the death of your wonderland.
The wounds are too raw to deal with the
Lifelessness you left behind: the corpse of Christmas.
I'll find a no-man's-land again.
I stand on the threshold thinking of other doors:
Clicked to with the softest of tiny clicks
Grinned round   tiptoed past
Thrown open   bustled through
Slammed in haste   flung wide in welcome
Opened onto a new life shut with a sigh.

No – it's not too soon. You've gone.
I must open the door on this winter wasteland.
Your skeleton of a room needs attention. Needs burying.
You've moved on – so must I.
There are new doors to be opened
But the rooms beyond won't ever replace yours.
I'll close it up
And lock it firmly into place until we meet.

Wherever you go, whatever you do
Our door will always be open to you.
However early, however late.

Independent Ian

Na, when I reached eighteen
Me 'ome was not my scene.
I needed freedom like, you know,
And life. Know what I mean?

I wanted to break out
Clear out of my old 'ome.
I wanted to leave Mum and Dad
And live life on me own.

I went in for this flat
With three of my best mates.
We 'ad to do it up a bit
It weren't 'alf in a state.

We made this small mistake
We did, me and the lads.
We mangled up the painting, like,
And 'ad to call our dads.

They grumbled, but they came
And did a lovely job.
And as us lads was in the way
We went down to the pub.

Our cooking's really bad,
Well, cooking is for girls,
And I don't like those take-aways
They make my stomach whirl.

And so I eat at Mum's
Three evenings if I can.
Yeah, no-one cooks chips like my Mum
She's magic with that pan.

And then I go to Mum's
On Sundays, for the day.
I love 'er Yorkshire pudding, yeah,
And roast beef done 'er way.

My washing I take 'ome
On Friday night each week.
Mum irons it crisp and lovely, like,
My shirts come back a treat.

Sometimes I'm short of cash
Dad helps me out always.
'E writes cheques with that strangled look
'Is eyes go sort of glazed.

But I don't mind – it's great!
Living this way is fab.
I'm independent now, you see.
I don't need Mum and Dad!

Slim Jim

I'm as thin as a rake
For I never eat cake
Don't like puddings or pastries or pies.
I'm as tall as a pole
Not a sweet-eating soul
Chocolates, ices, jam tarts, I despise.

But what's heaven to me
And a true luxury
Is a sandwich that's cut fat and thick.
Filled with cheese or with ham
Peanut butter or jam
Doesn't matter - they all go as quick.

Any day of the week
Just a sandwich I seek
I can manage one hail, rain or shine.
Punctuate the whole day
In my crust-chewing way
Wholemeal bread filled with cheese tastes divine.

At the dawn, late at night
Just a sandwich is right
Buttered thickly, the bread cut in hunks.
So don't give me a pud
For they do you no good.
Just a sandwich will do. Ready? Thanks!

Killerton

This was a favourite place
Visited each Spring:
A backdrop of pine and beech
Magnolias painted onto a cobalt background
And a grey-green foreground where daffodils shone.
We laughed and talked so much we didn't
Hear the birdsong.

After long dark days primroses were special.
Last year you sat on the rockery steps
Among primroses,
Smiled as I took your photo.

Today rooks caw from their towers.
I stand rooted
Watching the train in the valley
Travel too quickly away.

Returning

The swarm of orange lights invading far and wide
Dries up, vanishes like a mirage.
Southwards now: past the Malverns,
High, mysterious, mauve in the moonlight;

Past gold-lit spires, needles piercing the navy night,
And Cheltenham church, lit like a lighthouse;
Past the Cotswolds, swept by moonshine.
Bristol, the turning point: here peace begins.

the last time he saw her she was standing at her gate

He thunders down the blue vein of the motorway
Towards the heartland, to live again.
Mendips and Blackdowns, moongilded,
Sail by. His heart thuds: nearly there, nearly –

she had waved goodbye as he turned the corner

A glimpse of searchlight moon uncovers silver
Networked skinny lanes running over hills.
Headlights are swallowed up by night,
Blue skeins of miles unroll and disappear.

Moonbeams guide the familiar way, until at last
He is hugged by the soft green arms,
The loving embrace, of Devon.
Enfolded, he steers for home, lit by stars.

she had smiled her love when she kissed him goodbye

His house stands like a silent harbour:
Flooded by moonlight; sprinkled by starlight.
Ripples of sound wash up from the wood:
The bark of a far-off fox; the call
And answer of owls slicing the silence.

she had farewell tears brimming in her eyes

The cord of memory he has held onto unravels,
Pulls, tightens across his throat.
Tears that have brimmed in his heart for days,
For years, rise up to choke him. And he drowns.

Crossing The Waters

Casting off they leave the land
Sail from the harbour
Across the estuary
Into new waters.

They embarked freely
Knowing the dangers
But still they went
Choosing the ocean.

This is the journey
We all must make.
Away from the harbour
To the open seas.

After the London Bombs (7ᵗʰ July 2005)

(For our son who lives in London)

Today there's bustle in the house
With beds to make and food to buy.
Not any food, but all the best:
Tonight we have a special guest
Put flowers on his bedroom chest
And in the hall and any room
That needs a smiling July bloom.
We've washed and polished everything
And tweaked it all, like a new pin.
We've organised some things to do:
A walk; some golf – a round or two;
His friends and family to see.
Oh, how lovely it will be!
Today all clocks' hands seem stuck fast:
Despite the bustle, hours won't pass.
Can't wait – can't wait! Although he's grown,
Tonight our boy is coming home.

Happiness
(For our daughter)

A sunny day
Little to do
But sit and chat
And be with you.

A Woman's Work

Duty Calls

Gave	Gave	Gave	Gave
baby	Mum	Darren	Dad
her	her	some	dry
feed	pills	water	sheets

Society expects

Gave	Gave	Gave	Gave
baby	Mum	Darren	Dad
clean	her	his	his
nappies	bath	sandwiches	breakfast

that every woman

Gave	Gave	Gave	Gave
baby	Mum	Darren	Dad
her	a	his	his
bath	jab	tea	supper

will do

Gave	Gave	Gave	Gave
baby	Mum	Darren	Dad
her	her	his	his
feed	Horlicks	cocoa	pills.

her duty.

Housewife's Dream

Pop the washing in the washer
Dishes have their own machine
Push the plug in for the vacuum
Swiftly makes the house look clean.
Turn the tap on for the kettle
Flick the toaster on for toast
Slip the food into the micro
For a speedy, tasty roast.

Life's so simple and so easy
Open up your lucky prize
Packaged here in all disguises
Magic works before your eyes.

My great-grandma, if she came here,
How she'd stare in great surprise
Seeing all these undreamed wonders
She would not believe her eyes.

Today's Menu

We don't like the Beef Bourguignon
They don't like Sole Veronique.
The Quiche Lorraine
Went down the drain
And after kebabs we don't speak.

They quite liked the devilled chicken
But hated paprika goulash.
They won't touch prawns
Eggs Mornay scorn
And we all loathed the spiced-lamb hash.

They're fed up with eating salads.
Beef Wellington gives them the pip.
I know what they'd like
For supper tonight –
A nice plate of egg and chips!

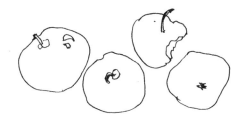

Mr Apple

Your Apple's a two-sided chappie
For he's sharp or he's sweet in his taste
He's crunchy and crisp and all juicy
So good not a morsel you'll waste.

Mr. Apple's a smart shiny dresser
Red or green he glows, topped by a stalk
All mushy he turns should you mention
His favourite dish, Sunday Pork.

He's really a versatile fella
And he'll bring you a host of surprises
He'll hide in a pie or a pudding
You'll find that he wears many guises.

He gets in a stew over custard
Or a smart coat of posh crisp meringue
But gets along well with the blackberries
And helps them when they're in a jam.

Don't talk about salads – it's dicey
Though he'll mix in the oven with fruit
He loves meeting all sorts of cheeses
And wearing new jackets of croûte.

He'll pop in your pocket so friendly
Lovely home in the orchard will please
His health can be drunk the World over
He'll travel long journeys with ease.

Once met, you cannot live without him
So enchanting his taste, smell and sight
At lunch, dinner, tea or at snack time
His company will always be right.

Feather Duster

I'd be lost without my duster,
Or tickling stick to you,
With its long bamboo cane handle
And its feathery top, bright blue.

It reaches into those parts
That I can never reach.
I can tickle the spiders' chins
And don't have to bend or stretch.

For tackling all those cobwebs
It really is a boon
With a few deft swipes about me
I can quickly clean a room.

My skirting's always gleaming
Since I bought my feathered friend.
I'm the envy of the cleaners
Who live around this end.

I really recommend one
Wish I'd bought one before.
It makes light work of your lampshades
And dusting's a feather-weight chore.

Wet Day

It's been a wet day.
No rain, but washing
      self
      teeth
      clothes
      vegetables
      floors
      windows
      dog
      dishes
      hair
      children

You can't get through one day without water.
Cheers!

Soap

I've been using soap for years
But still haven't come to grips with it.

Our Garage

Our garage is a double
And someone's taken trouble
To cram it floor to ceiling
With things we might be needing.
There's: Three old trikes
    Rusty bikes
    Tins of nails
    Holey pails
    Cracked a lot
    Plastic pots
    One dead scooter
    Someone's hooter
    Greasy candles
    Starting handles
    Toilet rolls
    Bags with holes
    Old sea shells
    Boots as well
    Battered caps
    Too-tight taps
    Garden tools
    Paddling pools
    Roller skates
    Roofing slates
    Broken bricks
    Pans non-stick
    Window panes
    Bamboo canes
    Paints in jars, but
    No cars.
Quelle disgrace
There's no space!

Sewing Bee

Stretch your mind like elastic
Peer with button-bright eyes
Snap up new ideas
Cotton on quickly
Get it taped
Be zippy
See eye to eye
Stick to the point –

Cut it out.

The Gentle Art

"Do you enjoy cooking, Kit?"
"Well, I like it quite a bit."
"Now, I love it and I can't wait
To get my hands on that hot-plate.
I could spend my entire day
Passing hours in this way:

       Beating up eggs
       Chopping off legs
       Crushing crabs' claws
       Stuffing hens' maws
       Pounding up steak
       Beheading skate
       Skewering meat
       Impaled so neat
       Grinding up lamb
       Slicing thick ham
       Cutting pork thin
       Tearing off skin.

It's such fun and it's so thrilling!
Hard work too." — "Yes, it sounds killing."

Preparing Supper

Millions of hands at this minute
Preparing millions of meals.
Millions of hands over millions of years have
Prepared millions of meals.

Millions of mothers, mothers of millions
For millions of years, move over.
Make someone else make it
Tonight.

Teatime Scoreboard

And here is tonight's teatime scoreboard:

Slices of Toast 2	Scrambled Eggs 2
Scone-of-the-West 1	Spoons of Jam 2
Butterfly Cake 1	Dundee Cake 0
Bakewell Tart 0	Granny Smith 1

Match between Yoghurt and Ice Cream postponed
Because of severe icing.

Dilemma

I've fallen in love with a limestone floor
It's ever so, ever so nice.
As soon as I saw its strong, handsome face,
I was head over heels in a trice.

It's gorgeously smooth, deliciously cool,
So mellow and friendly but tough.
No – now I look closer it seems to be
Quite well-worn and horribly rough.

It's terribly cold. It's terribly old.
Oh, what am I going to do?
For now I can see that this ancient floor
Will always remind me of you!

To Mary

Dear Mary,

      Sorry that I didn't write
      Things here have been pretty quiet
      Did you hear about Jack's leg?
      Had it off – he's got a peg
      Simon has just had the mumps
      Sally's head to foot in lumps
      Fido's looking rather strange
      Pussy's had that awful mange
      Aunt Flo's going round the bend
      Rupert's broken leg won't mend
      Central heating's on the blink
      Can't unblock the kitchen sink
      Telly went up bang in smoke
      Father's cracking lurid jokes
      Michael's having an affair
      With a girl with golden hair
      Mabel's broken her glass eye
      Can't stop drinking, though she tries
      Mr. Browning's just as bad
      Gillie Postlethwaite's gone mad
      Mrs. Clifford-Smyth-White's son's
      Taking drugs – says it's such fun
      Tina Banks has tried all cures
      To remove those spots of hers
      Mrs. Braithwaite's lost her wig
      Ian's moved out into digs
      Angie Philpott's getting wed
      Marrying that awful Fred.
      As I say, not much to tell,
      Love as always,
            Auntie Nell.

Revision

Between the covers she carefully placed a lifetime:
Their christenings, birthdays, Christmases,
Marriages and children of their own.
Images of friends, parties, holidays
Jostled through the years,
Thronging as deep as drifts of autumn leaves.

Now she lies, blind at eighty
Beneath the covers
Seeing it all.

Birdie

In black velvet she hops into the lift
Sweeps her cloak across one shoulder
And twitters.
Blue eyes, thin white hands, fuchsia mouth
Tweet together
As she frantically presses the button.

She talks of smart-set things
In her smart-set way.
Nineteen to the dozen she chirrups
Claw fingers ruffling across her velvet plumage
Inside her black leather bag
Across her rows of pearls.
Head on one side she asks questions but
Eyes rolling and darting
Doesn't care about the answers.

Third floor.
The doors slide open.
Breathless with chatter she flutters to her office
Surreptitiously adjusting her smart blond wig
As she flies down the corridor
To her nest.

Memorable Women

You never see women look nowadays
As they did, when I was a girl.
They were all so old and immensely fat,
They had glaring eyes that would stare, like cats',
Had a brood of snotty-nosed ugly brats
To threaten, when I was a girl.

You never hear women speak nowadays
As they did, when I was a girl.
They bawled news abroad, spreading tales of ours,
By their gates they stood, screeching loud for hours
To the street at large, with ear-splitting powers.
No secrets, when I was a girl.

You never see women dress nowadays
As they did, when I was a girl.
To hide all those curlers, a turban, tight,
Those broad bunioned feet, slippered, looked a sight.
And a wrap-around pinny was just right,
De rigueur, when I was a girl.

You never see faces look nowadays
As they did, when I was a girl.
They looked grim always, and they frightened me:
Opening wide big mouths, only gums you'd see.
Could a face so creased someone's mother's be?
So ugly, when I was a girl.

You never see women here nowadays
As you did, when I was a girl.
I've looked everywhere and they're not around,
But I think I know where they can be found:
Tucked up sleeping peacefully underground,
Like joy, when I was a girl.

War Widow

Though you're dead and gone
To me you live on
And I carry this flag in your name.

Though you're dead I'll fight
In this endless night
And I carry this wreath in your name.

Though you're dead to me
Living here you'll be
For I carry the love of your name.

Though you're dead in war
You'll live as before
For I carry your child with your name.

42

Ghostly Remains

She was at a table for one
Fiddled with her sherry glass
"Malcolm let me copy his snooker game, Mum, and tonight I'm…"
Fingered her two rows of pearls
Silently ate her hors d'oeuvre
Straightened her glasses
"Debbie Sanderson says I can go to tea tomorrow, Mum. Can I?"
Smoothed her blue-rinsed, tight short curls
Downcast eyes on her steak.
"Had to go to March today. Saw Chris Henderson. He said…"

What a noise they make!
Absently toyed with her coffee spoon.
Thought about Vanessa, dead at twenty;
Toby, killed in the war;
Dear Jack, had a heart attack, died ten years ago.
"What shall we do tomorrow? If it's fine we could…"
Paid her bill. Slipped on her coat.
Seems only yesterday
That she was part of a family too.
Glided out unnoticed
Quiet as a ghost.

Good Night

Kick off the cares
Pull off the problems
Unbutton the frustrations
Step out of the troubles
Slip off the pettiness
Peel off the disappointments
Unhook the anxieties
Push down the rows
Brush out the unhappiness
Switch off the hours
Shut out the dark.

Late Garden

Now there's a lovely garden, she said,
And we stopped to admire the riot of
Geraniums, late roses, dahlias and golden rod.
Too showy for me, but she loved colour
Especially on a sunny day.
Things look better in the sunshine, she said.

Small things to gladden her dull heart,
Grown grey with age.

The Life Cycle of the Greater Spotted Ball Gown

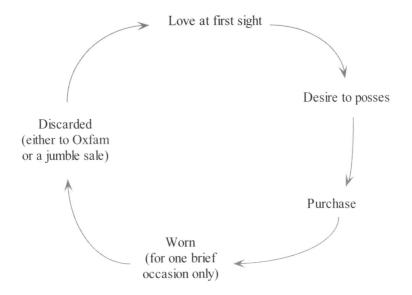

Mother's Clothes

My wardrobe's full of clothes
I've had for years and years.
Old coats quite tattered
Shoes so battered
Such frightful things, my dears.

There's lots and lots of hats
Now all quite out-of-date.
Old worn-out blouses
Baggy trousers
In colours that I hate.

I thought I'd throw them out.
They really ought to go
To jumble sales, or
Oxfam shops, or
As gifts for Auntie Flo.

It's sad to part with them
Although it's plain to see
They've had their ration
Grown old-fashioned
Yes, just the same as me.

The Weak-willed Slimmer

One biscuit, two biscuits
Three biscuits, four.
Five biscuits, six biscuits
Seven biscuits,
More.....

Sad Thoughts in the Chip Shop

How skilfully she does it
She flips in first the fish
Then deftly turns into the bag
A golden mound of chips.

There's nothing smells so English
As good old fish and chips
A dash of salt and vinegar
The lick of greasy lips.

When I was only little
We asked for piece and four.
That tiny shop was chock-a-block
The queue miles from the door.

And sometimes after Brownies
Before we all went home
We'd ask for thruppence worth of chips
Open, held in a cone.

With thruppence worth of pleasure
Homewards we ate our chips
A thing we often did those days
Of unconsidered hips.

But now we have them rarely
Cholesterol you see.
They cost a lot, they make you fat
Most pleasures do - pity!

Enjoy Yourself

"And we'll bend and stretch, bend and stretch.
That's it. Count to ten.
And we'll twist and turn, twist and turn.
Let's do that again."

Oh no! I really can't stand it
We've been at it now for years.
Just look at the time
Only half-past nine
Another hour. Oh dear.

My feet are starting to panic
My knees are going under.
My neck's locked tight
And we all look a sight
As round the room we blunder.

Oh! Look at poor Mrs. Braithwaite
I really think she's fainted.
Has she hit her head?
No – I think she's dead
Such a deathly pallor she's painted.

"Now, now, Mrs. Clifford-Smythe-White
You shouldn't do that, my dear.
You're too old you know
To skip about so
You'll do some damage, I fear."

And awful Angela Philpotts!
Just look at that leotard.
She's plenty of curves
But it's so absurd
To squeeze them all in quite so hard.

Oh, not again! I can't manage
To run on the spot once more
Or stretch to my toes
Or reach down my nose
To touch my knees on the floor.

Practice for next week?
I can hardly stand up straight.
– Oh yes, I feel fine
Had a lovely time
See you next week – don't be late!

Celebration

Tonight the moon is a ripe apricot
Hanging over the lavender wall of the sea.
Tawny moonbeams tread with slippery
Soft-soled feet on the sea's rippling back
Massaging as it curls and stretches
Creams in the sultry navy night
Swish-swishes like a jaunty taffeta skirt
Jouncing from side to side.

Along the lace-capped shore they stroll
Feeling stout with robust Italian food
July strawberries and clotted cream
Spumy champagne sparkling with shooting stars
And frothy cappuccino hot as Latin hedonism.
Before dinner she opened the gifts he gave her
Leaping heart fizzing with bubbles of excitement.

The afternoon was full of lazing in the sundrenched garden
With their cats sprawled deeply asleep hidden like shipwrecks
In the deepest emerald shadows of the herbs.
She read in the arbour – cool, submerged – beneath sea-green arches of
Buttery honeysuckle and sprays of foaming white jasmine.
At her feet stood a grey-coated army of ancient warriors
Upholding lavender spears as they waded in a
Dazzling lime-starred alchemilla ocean that
Ebbed and flowed along the margin of the path.
Whispering leaves nodded secrets back and forth overhead
And a kaleidoscope of rainbow birdsong sprinkled the air.

They had lunch in sapphire shade under the parasol
Fat lemon brie, creamy marbled stilton
Sun-oranges streaming marigold juice
Plump downy-cheeked terracotta peaches
After the morning's bustle of people phone calls work.

She felt like an enchanted princess
When he woke her with a birthday kiss.
The sky shone saffron as she swam up
Through shoals of spells and waves of dreams to
Burst the black surface of sleep.
He had lovingly placed beside her
A pale-scented pink-faced New Dawn rose
To start her own short span of ordinary magic.

Sidmouth Fever

(with apologies to John Masefield)

I must go down to the Radway again, to the vast and silvery screen,
And all I ask is Colin Firth; the best thing I've ever seen,
And a choc ice and a coffee and my neighbour snoring,
And the phone calls and the catcalls when the film gets boring.

I must go down to the front again, for the gulls are there swarming high,
And pick my way through chip bags and the beer cans rolling by;
And all I ask is a clear path through the cars that are racing,
And a warm coat and a thick rug for the wind is – bracing.

I must go down to the sea again, where the waves crash big and strong:
Here I can see a small young me and days that were sunny and long.
Now all I ask is gin in a flask and a deckchair to steer me by,
And a quiet beach and a long sleep under a dreamless sky.